Seeing The Desert Green

COVER PHOTOGRAPH BY GEORGE CURTSINGER

LATITUDES PRESS Since 1966
Robert Bonazzi, Editorial Director
Elizabeth Griffin-Bonazzi, Publisher

Distributed by Latitudes
Post Office Box 613
Mansfield, Texas 76063
Or Call (817) 472-7737

ACKNOWLEDGEMENTS

Grateful acknowledgement is made to the editors of the
following publications where these poems--many of
which have been revised--first appeared.

Anima
Cedar Rock
Earthwise
Embers
Forum
Manhattan Poetry Review
Passages North
The Pegasus Review
The Poet
Poetry Newsletter
Shenandoah
Southern Humanities Review
Studia Mystica
Williamette Journal of the Liberal Arts

Sybil Estess

Seeing The Desert Green

Latitudes Press

Since 1966

CONTENTS

PART I

PART II

PART III

For Ted

PART I

MASSAGE ON CHRISTMAS EVE

The country club's masseur teaches night courses
in sensuous, not ''sensual,'' massage.
His French accent thick as Creme Brulee, explains that
''Sensuous is not the same as sex, mesdames, messieurs;
something more: the body. . .healing by hands.
More potent than medicines, n'est-ce pas?''

In his last class, like Noah,
Monsieur masseur groups us in twos, male-female.
Stripped to bikinis and g-strings,
we stretch face down on towels.
With my back to him, I never know my partner's name.
Yet for two nights, we touch unlike timid new lovers do:
compulsively, in ten-minute effleurages,
petrissages, frictions, roving from ribs
to buttocks to knee-backs, from forearms to fingers. . .
taking turns with the touching.

Later that year, when Mother comes to spend Christmas,
this silent night before the fire,
I'll give her one early gift,
before bells begin in downtown churches at midnight.

At first as a matter of course,
she won't have it.
Says it's too cold to take off her clothes,
that she can't lie still for ten minutes,
that rubbing would hurt the crick in her neck.

Even so, she dares to disrobe
and stand before me nearly naked.
All clocks count slowly backward.
Under my spell,
Mother lets me examine her thin body,
its hunched back and scattered, brown fibrous moles.
I hold the cold cocoanut oil in my palm to warm it,
then begin massaging her waist, as he told us.
I rub her hips lightly, above the pelvis,
which he said not to miss.
Moving up, I arrive at the spot
she says is her tensions: her neck.
She talks, says I'm doing it wrong, wrong,
and asks me questions I don't try to answer.

I move slowly to her shoulders, her upper arms,
thin-skinned, flabby.
At the wrists, I feel protruding bones
that will be there long after her skin is gone.
I finger the soft, blue veins,
the brown age spots on her hands.
I massage each crooked finger,
each long fingernail, painted red.
I rub and rub the rough scalp
under her coarse brown and gray hair.

I descend to her torso,
things, backs of her knees,
tips of her long, cold, arthritic feet.
My hands touch all ten painted toes.

Finally, the last four minutes are silence.
She's face down: no place to go.
In cathedrals, midnight mass is beginning.
The priests are serving,
to parishioners in their power.
Eucharist has its healing effect:
eating the dead host to unwrap it
by that yeasty ritual.

After this, can we consume each other again? Or
have hands healed us of all the old blames?
Are we two Marys, anointing one of our bodies for death?
Hunched over these bones that bore me,
I keep vigil at midnight
under moons making the windows silver
against brass by flames that illumine
my hands.

RIVER'S NORTH FORK

I did not like moving this far.
Here near the glacier where we are reminded
how anything on earth can freeze too early:
gardens, berries, roots, love.

In the summer, so far north,
the sun was constant, hot as Africa's.
By winter solstice this September cold
will be so deadly dark.

Under the moon last night we drifted into winter.
Snow crept. Morning is silent and still.

SPRING DEATH

The father hurts more than
his life allows.
He dies protesting.
His vision, once perfect,

grows strange. His hospital breath
is pure oxygen,
faking the life-flame,
making it burn.

Revived, his eyes
see his grown daughter,
then don't see her.
The first day

he manages to say,
"This time I almost went."
The second he demands
she tell him if there is hope.

Told, in evening, nothing holds.
Unmanned, he wheezes,
"Get my pill. . .please. The squirrels
are out early this year.

It's Febru. . . ." Not true.
It is already March.
There are no squirrels.
The third night

his last words were
to his wife:
"Who are you?"

RACHEL WEEPS

Laura Estess
1963-1983

"A voice was heard . . .
Rachel weeping for her children. . . ."
                            --Jeremiah

Why the magi cart gold
we can imagine: all births
are regal--that of Rachel's

children, and the Christ-child.
Even the man who murdered
Laura. We comprehend frankincense, for

fathers offer their offspring
to God. But why myrrh?
To bear the stench of what

each cradle rocks? Old Mother,
your cries in Ramah reach beyond
ears in sacked Judah. Your wails echo

for all innocence that madmen will slay
through the ages. They mock birth, even
on Epiphany Feast, the day she died.

TWO FROM LAUREL

He is a farmboy, good with numbers,
who wants to be an accountant. In Chicago
there is a school
that can teach him. She, from Laurel,
plays the frenchhorn in her father's church
and draws sketches.

Her dad doesn't like sketches;
his dad knows no numbers.
Her dad says, "Go to church."
His dad says, "Where's Chicago?
If it's north of Laurel,
boy, you don't need school."

For that contest to art school
she draws many sketches--
better than any other girl's in Laurel.
Like the numbers
he knew, they can win her Chicago--
take her from church.

One Sunday before church
she burns the note from the art school.
(It had come from Chicago
saying "first prize for your sketches.")
Both daddys say "No." But he clings to numbers,
and schools himself--meets her in Laurel.

At their wedding in Laurel
they marry in her father's church.
She never understands the numbers
he loves; rarely speaks of art school.
He seldom mentions the sketches
she hides. Each mourns the loss of Chicago.

Neither one goes to Chicago;
they live in Laurel
while she dreams sketches,
keeps going to church.
One day he dies. She enters art school,
remembers how he'd loved numbers.

The second school prizes her sketches,
but she is a lonely number (one, only) in Laurel.
She sees his face in each church all the way to Chicago.

GRANDMOTHER POEM

Thirty years after your stroke,
you arise in a dream
as a brown Amazon friend.
I go all the way out to your lonely hut--
a hard trip--to see how you've lasted.

Your long hair is unbound, a primitive queen's.
Your bare, bony feet touch southern soil.
I watch you draw well-water, fill old gourds.
I follow you in your sweltering world.
At fifty you are old as

Methuselah's wife.
Your life is sun-ups, sun-downs.
Between each light, toil.
You seldom speak.
Breakfast is chickens.

killed at dawn.
In the corn crib you strike a rattler.
At the wood stove,
you sweat in August dog-days.
Promethean, you heat irons

for your ironing by fire.
I hear you scream
when you step in red-hot coals
under your scalding washpots.
Although I run dusty miles toward help,

the bad burn never heals.
I hold the blue-ring churn steady while you doze.
"It's a sin to laugh," you always say.
Old puritan grandmother,
you tell me you want to leave me

your gold wedding band.
You were young, joking,
last night when we whispered unfinished murmurings
all through the moon.
Ring on my hand,

I dance with you, limping, till dawn.

HISTORIES

Here in this electric kitchen, myths died.
Baby, asleep in Vicks vapor and antibiotics,
what boxtop shall I peel off for you?

My dad rode miles on mules to school.
Ran home when he saw a white cloud.
Mamaw taught him to fear:

storms, wild women--whose breasts covered the moon
out the window covering the barn--
swimming (he might go naked), and basketball.

Mother's papa preached Pentecostal hell.
Hell and hominy grits with clabber
were all she knew night-time was.

Her life caravaned to California
for gold
fields holding work.

But no narratives are left, little one.
I rode in wagons
only when your great granddaddy took me.

I was three when he died. Daddy sold cars.
Listen, my only child,
even old stories can't report hearts.

Father. Mother. Son.
Chipping off, like icebergs,
now we drift.

SEPTEMBER MOURNING

We lived six states apart. I did not see you
often enough, so I put your picture up
over my desk. You offer the same smile
prevailing through loss of your daughter, your
crippling polio, the cancer that took you.

Now, a year later, I learn just by chance
which September day you fell. Not knowing
you had died, I thought all our air turned
too thick for breathing. I knew, somehow,
we'd lost you. I kept thinking I'd call. . . .

Anne, when I sensed you sweep over the coast
of Carolina last September, I believed you ascended
by a buoying roll-call of your trials--gone.
Untriumphed, we trudge with that lumpy weight
in our bodies: your absence going on.

DIRECTIONS

Kayla Broussard
1969-1978

You knock at my back door in April.
You're the skinny, curly-haired girl
who once lived here.
You want to see your old house,
the pool where you learned to swim.

You were only four then.
At nine, out of school,
you ride your new bike,
drop it, hop in, floor-flop.
You struggle over four rooms--

on one leg.
Cancer in your small bones.
Your folks believe in being found
in Christ. I've seen what it costs.
Doctors' bills come to my mailbox, lost.

When I first walked in this house
signs on the walls said,
"He is Resurrection,"
"Easter is Always."
You played our old church organ

that day, later pumped with one leg,
tried "Jesus Saves" on the piano--
looked about you, crawled out.
It's been three days since you said,
"Where is death, mama?

When I go there
will God help me walk."

20

TRYING TO EXORCISE: GRAND CANYON

Since she left him, she confuses directions.
In the Southwest, she can't be here or there right.
She dreams of Northeast and her lover.
She runs from something serpentine;
he is the snake.

Yesterday she saw sleek Aspen
and said it was no real compensation for birch.
A late waker, today she can't stop sleeping fast enough.
The 4:45 alarm
pounces as he did.

She's prey inside jeans,
wool socks for this cold.
To see desert sunrise,
she hugs ground where she is:
glad to be West,

waiting by the old, coiled Canyon's south rim.

DISCONNECTION IN SANTA BARBARA

He's left other places.
Her place seems o.k. to leave.
He thinks of it as soil he can return to.
He thinks of being invited,
from time to time, to come back.
He thinks lovers like habitual return.

Brushfires occur as the dry season comes.
He worries, of course.
He hears that one wind blackened her canyon.
There are long rainy times.
Mudslides. Some foundations give way.
Now he knows how quick she is
to find a new house.

STAINED GLASS

This Baptist church is her history:
marriages, immersions, death.
So like her to hope and hold to memory.
She wore a white dress
when they buried her husband,
requested the choir to sing,
"He's the fairest of ten thousand to my soul."

In stained glass she designed
a bird with ivory wings,
blue water below.
Above Him, blue-stained air.
In between them,
the frozen, green rind of earth.
The sun's four gold rays reach down
to tell us in these dark pews
we are healed.

Her gift awakens old notions
of Holy Ghost in some form--a dove.
This window is like one "at St. Peter's," she says.
I think of how Peter was like her
and like all of us:
needing soul to join betraying body.
Untouched by this descending,
soft and white flight,
never whole.

THE GEESE

They have an autumn pattern, a southern place
in fall. They know circles everywhere.

They form triangles and seem sure their honks
are heard by each other. They trust tomorrow

will be the same steady air. We know a thousand
threats could counter them in their plan. Yet, envy them

Geese launch the same October every year.

PART II

AGÍA GALÍNI
(Southern Crete: 1983)

Like vultures bending over bones,
old women in black hover and squat to pick dry greens
shriveled by July heat
and light so bright that we veil with umbrellas, sunglasses, shawls.

Pines and cypress once shadowed this island.
Now bent olive trees rattle in wind-gusts that won't stop.
At noon in Vorízia,
I watch an old man, cursing, wash parts of an olive press.
"Some people leave home to see what they can become,"
I imagine he says.
He does not.
But Kazantzákis left, and Theotokopolis--
unlike this mother who leads an ass bearing her baby, waterjugs, dust

I've crossed oceans for the town Agía Galíni (Holy Serenity)
to see one cat stalk trash pails behind a cafe
where John Denver sings songs (cut in L.A.) about Colorado.
Here bare-breasted British, Norwegian, German girls sun themselves
as if Apollo can't go as far north as their misty seas.

Then at Knossós,
we tramp on the continent's oldest road
while Anna from Oxford, tired of med school, cleans rooms,
then picks field tomatoes
when the restless settle after the season these waiters hate.
Like blonde, pregnant Helena from Copenhagen,
who owns our cheap pension,
Anna is hooked by her dark, Greek fisherman.

26

For twenty-one nights, I imagine
Aphrodite rising in starry air over these ancient waters.
But even Zeus, born in the cave on Mt. Díkti,
fled long ago with Europa
who had said *adio* to Phoenicia.

Like many of us,
deities seldom sit quietly at home.

"Return soon," the telegram at the one-room P.O. says. So
those contented friends back by the fires call and call
to ask what we find when we go so far
away from them--just as we would ask the old gods.
All they could say is what
we must know: "We can't answer, can't come back."

MASTODON TEETH

Orange coral, tan sea-cork, fishnets
hang in curves over the formica bar
of his hermit hut, the man from Racine,
a curator who's lived for seven years
on this beach-cliff in south Texas.
He scavenges the coral from the Caribbean,
perhaps Cancun. He shows us petrified wood,
as we fight off troops of mosquitos,
the fields of Texas expanding beyond us,
the ''Danger''-marked sea below. . . .
Three pieces he holds off until the end--
two five-inch mastodon teeth, one mammoth's bone.

The teeth are encrusted with nipple-like cusps
that make them bumpy and ugly and odd.
They aren't at all like teeth of a toy elephant,
or glassed, dated relics in some museum.
No, real mastodon teeth simply lie
in my quaking hands--casual remains of a monster,
picked up on an inaccessible shoreline
near Brazoria. The man keeps them with
a foot-long piece of the old pachyderm's bone.

Dear old beachcomber, you loosed fear in me
on that hot and itchy night under an August moon.
Fangs gnawed in my kneading nightmares,
and I waked knowing this: of all there was
of these beasts, only their teeth remain.

SUNSET ON THE BAYOU

for the Challenger seven

Now dusk is on Houston: flat and breastless.
Not on Seattle, red-hilled Greensboro,
nor Concord, Kona, old Jerusalem--
those subtle or volcano slopes they could have climbed.

It's the last of January, virginal
until last Tuesday. It's 5:30,
six weeks past winter solstice.
Soft southern deadness, broomstrawed and brown.

Sun, setting we say, is red placenta, edging
the child's promised sky not yet night. . . .
Walking one block from my house,
I'm by the concreted, graffiti-marked bayou, circling this city,

churning rain debris, turtles, trash, tires,
unfound trapped bones--a woman's who drove off
in last year's rainstorm catastrophe.
Stars, boats, babies, all that goes forth here
will travel again--down, down such dark canals.

THE COUNTRY IDIOT

After "The Village Idiot"
by Edward Hirsch

Not many remember him anymore, my cousin
who had epileptic fits in the bottoms of holes
and other abysses he had to be in
by necessity--like the life he was in
with no means to control. No medicine
that they could pay for or wanted to know about
for their son named Leon in that land, at that time.
Now that he is little more than a vague memory,
I still see the country men taunt him
to climb down the fresh-dug well
late that night. He swallowed his tongue
and his mouth foamed
when the loud crowd turned its head. I remember
the giggles, the jests, and how he grinned afterward,
as if having come through some trial,
some accomplishment. And it was:
his mere living. Another extravagance
from my red rural past--like my grandmother's house
with no bathroom, no electricity;
like the king snake she found in her dresser drawer once.
And like Leon's two brothers, also dead: one in a carwreck
drunk doing ninety; the other burned
in the gasoline housefire.
(He only wanted to clean the paintbrushes
near the heater.) Each grave has a picture put by their
mother, my aunt. I was seven
and fresh from town when I fled,
so late, from Leon in black water
to grandmother's bedside for her to cover
my eyes from Leon whom I hated,
Leon, who never missed Sunday School
once in his thirty-one years. Full mid-moons,
now I fear him.

OLYMPIC COAST

Here where they looked out for enemies
from 1904 till 1953,
a white-and-green sloop glides, glides
going its easy direction.
One man paddles a small boat, slowly as a snail crawls.

Indigo waves softly splash the white
coastguard lighthouse, a placid guide, beaming
bright red, red, red.
Oh look! Clouds break on slumbering Mt. Baker
always shrouded in white.
See how today we believe

northwestern volcanoes and rain
will stay in abeyance.
This crystalline, trusty air calms all July.
No 1942-type December snipers
will take us. Or serpents lull and
then coil in mid-summer grass.

IN MISSOULA, SNOWED-IN

Outside in the December storm,
snow falls like salt drowning in saltiness.
For eons it's been like this--
ground white as satin in caskets.
Everything hushed. . . .

One train goes East
leaves Hoernor Waldorf's lumber mill,
winds across the Little Rockies toward Butte and
Bozeman. Its mopish whistle hollers
in Hellgate Canyon's windiest bend.

I burrow around her:
my house in the woods on Cherry Street,
light fires of store-bought apple and pine.
When the weatherman says, "Tonight it will clear,"
I think of how three Catholic priests,

two nervous oncologists,
many old millworkers whose shifts let out
at eleven, the ethics professor,
one poet just new on the wagon,
six sex therapists--all in therapy together--

a housewife, or a nurse will push open
clogged doors to shovel or snowblow walkways
under full moons and electric light.
I wonder if we will notice ghastly white peaks,
bowed tamarak bones beneath layers of new, white

cadaverous drapings. Will we imagine all those skulls
of Blackfeet or Kootenai Indians
and pioneer white men lying inert and
frozen under us? Two blocks away, one hamburger hovel
fries beef raised in the Mission Valley

or grown in the spring-buttercupped Bitterroot,
flown back in from Chicago. Next door, Safeway
sells little docked lambs which have been trucked
the same Highway 90. At the corner, neon lights
blink amid million-shaped flakes in this

hoary, white glare:
yellow and green and red.

MISSOULA BARS

In Stockmans
the crowd downs bourbon fast as bison were killed,
playing keno in hidden back rooms.
The Palace Hotel lobby holds talent contests for cowboys
on Monday nights.
At the Eastgate Bar
a blonde lady waiting tables gets a telephone call.
"Anybody here for a twelve-inch prick?" she yells back.
In The Cabin, out near the Clark Fork River,
the weariness here on this last frontier
is held off each Friday:
Jan Dell steps up in tightest white boots and red velvet.
There's a blue August sky.
All eyes are fixed,
all glasses raised at round tables
while she croons
the ecstatic first pure notes of "Stand By Your Man!"

GEORGE SEGAL'S "THE HOLOCAUST"

Sculpture outside of
Legion of Honor Museum
San Francisco

Even from this high distance,
the Pacific is green and turbulent.
Segal's eleven white bronzes
glow like seagulls in the lowering dark.

One survivor looks West, not seeing horizons,
only the charged barbed-wire fence.
Two women.
Eve--holding her bitten apple--rests

on Adam, or Adonis. The other naked
woman's hands shriek.
Her fingers stand straight up
as the hair on her head does--electrified.

Here are six men, plus Abram, repented.
All Israel's father tries to shield his son's eyes
from the horror.
Too late. Isaac (without a ram) crouches,

hands behind him, his feet tucked under.
He is already traded--this time to demons.
His sacrificed foot forms a cup
holding six daisies,

their stems bound in one fold of tinfoil.
The lone standing figure cannot cover these Jews,
the stump of his minyam.
I, no Sarah, Rachel, or Esther,

leave ten tribes of Jacob unburied,
exposed to this last, cold sea.

HURRICANE CAMILLE

Sixty miles inland, winds clock 200.
In the eye of it, stillness.
Before, after, we shut our ears all night.
My mother grips a Bible as trees fall,
breaking like sticks.

At 7:00 a.m. skies are El Greco green,
then bright blue as August dawns.
Our homes without light or water.
Everything hot.
But by the bay, the tidal wave rises fifty feet.

They find babies tied high to trees
by mothers who had hoped.

PART III

CHRISTMAS OF ORIGINS

For years I harassed my husband each Christmas:
a lioness clawing his back. Like shepherds,
I was afraid for another reason.
I was afraid we'd miss the joy of the season--
tree-trimming, shopping, baking, parties,
angelic music, Santa Claus, cards.

So this time he's tamed me.
He's placed the tree by our window early,
first day of Advent, lined up oratorios,
played Bach and Handel's *Messiah* for
fourteen days straight. I can't complain.

Instead, I tell him that back in my family
Mama, holiday soldier, tramped from store door
to store door for weeks,
marking off twenty-six relatives far away
to whom we must mail gifts.

Childlike, she displayed her gems one by one
to my sister and me after school,
calling off kinfolks' names,
wondering if they'd like this treasure or
if they already had one.

Then the pleasure of wrapping:
no red bow too small for her clockmaker hands.
Fifty gifts under the magic tree for a week
before she had to box them.

The rest were wonderfully ours.
Daddy, kidhearted, would peek, shake them,
peek again, say could we have just one
early. She'd answer "No." They'd go at it,
back and forth, about why or why not,
their young daughters watching with grins.

When Christmas Eve came, Mama'd surrender,
so then we'd have just one to open
early for four of us.
Daddy would never be satisfied, and
they'd go to bed like two friends

arguing over whether he could or couldn't
stand it till morning. Daybreak:
he was butler waiting with waffles,
strawberries for Christmas color, coffee
for her in her covers if she preferred.

Cameras clicked. I wanted, of course,
never to miss this annual happiness.
Since Daddy died, with one beat,
when they were each in their forties,
breaking a rhythm certain as metronomes set,

I keep thinking the way I learned it
from them: if one misses Christmas
there may not be next time
when their great joy would visit again.

WISHES AND NEEDS

Sometimes, I am born in Boston.
I come of age in old mansions,
bricked and blue-veined.

A Japanese garden
circles a sculptured pool.
Inspired by my mother, professor of Eastern art,

I attend Madame de Trop's school for girls.
At eighteen, trickles of Latin and Greek
and renaissance painting flow from my brain,

down the refined sinus track,
into my classic nose and out of
my seasoned mouth.

By twenty-one, I choose for proper reasons
to research allergies, or to conduct the Paris Pops.
Trim, each day I romp with African animals,

swim with Amazon fish from Brazil.
Then, piranha-like wishes are stilled.
Of real needs I write good poems.

At numberless parties, at last
entertained, I propose with perfect words,
the immaculate, right toast.

ONE MYTH

When Eve does it she does not think
it will come to this.
Hearing the gorgeous snake's voice,
she wants to join
the succulent tree, Adam's body,
even God. . .
Until now he's never seemed cunning.

Cast out, like Ophelia, she's mad.
Eons of birthing
don't end all the sadness.
Her big belly grows.
She calls out, alone, to the one she hears
laughing.

One day she'll dance, see in the distance
her daughters possess their gardens again.
In their own tongue
they absolve Eve of sin.

SEA DREAMS

Needs met,
my baby lies on my stomach, dozing--
doing the yogi's deep belly-breath,

At six weeks
two pounds heavier,
he can't return

to that sac where he swam.
Before he was born,
I dreamed of an ocean.

The green waves called me in
but I could not go.
Taking wrong roads up,

I saw the sea far, far down.
I wanted someone with me
to share this water:

husband, mother, sister, friend.
After his birth,
I take the forbidden swim.

Late afternoon, alone;
the ocean is dark, swift.
I make the wide-swung loop,

survive the undertow,
holding
my son above the deep.

FLIGHT

Sometimes halfway through workdays
I dream of taking you from nurseries
where you wait each dull day.

We flee south, south
toward the lapping, irregular sea.
Shedding routines like snakeskins,

we fling those monitored playtimes behind.
Son, I take you below time--
recall that day we dived?

We saw the coral, the sword-fish,
the octopus waving watery business
between them.

We tell their secondless secrets
now when we say
"Goodbye," "Goodbye."

NEED HOUR

3:00 a.m.
My best friend
from her grave says,
"I am buried alive."
Crash on the college ski-bus to Colorado Springs.
Choirs sing *La Mort des Enfants*
as they lower kids, live, underground--
nail them shut.
I shout "No!" in my dream.
       Tied to me by a tether,
       my son screams
       with some pain in the night.
       Connected, I fly out to rock,
       rock, rock,
       my tiny boy-child, we rock.
Next: the ski-bus I'm driving goes
out of control.
My late dream-themes recur:
No brakes when I drive from the back.
What is it like to be buried alive?
       No, not again.
       Now I'm too tired to go.
       Wait. . . . . "I gave him milk already."
       "You . . . what?"
       "Where is the other bottle?"
       "I don't know."
       "Why?"
       "Why not?"
       "Is he cold?" "Too hot?"
       "Shut out the light."
       "I think it's his stuffed nose again."

In darkness he holds out his arms to me
and both of us rock.
Twice he cries out to touch me.
How would he know those who rocked me have gone?
His cheek rests on mine.
This is the blood-bonding.
It is 4:00. Close his door.
Maybe we'll sleep--
who are our . . . where is
the Comforter?
I am your
Mother,
Father, Baby,
rock me.

THE BEACH: MOTHER AND CHILD

Destin, Florida

When I am a child,
white sand shapes more than castles.
I make cathedrals.
The white sea-foam is the host
I take in with my eyes for a secret, sacred
communion.

Thirty years later,
you mock my old, imagined, holy cosmos.
Son, you are just nineteen months
when you chastise this salty eucharist.

Seared early by mortal vanity,
at the edge of sand and sea elements,
you shake your small fist, crying, "No! No!"
as God and the ocean kiss and sin
against your barefoot toes.

DESERT REUNION

Alfalfa fields dance under Three Sisters,
snow-packed above us.
Hairy Sasquatch watches
as our memories ease:
your late lover, my miscarriages.
Time ceases its labor pangs.
Blood-red May poppies balloon
when your desert turns green.
Skimming pastures,
we two women friends,
saddleless, gallop in summer's new air. . . .
An Oregon moon.
June crickets' songs chirp and soothe.

DEJA VU IN TORQUAY

I

It starts across a war-torn Atlantic
in the 1940's in spared America
over thirty years before. One little girl hears
nursery rhymes in the young mother's lap.

They flap the favored pages again:
"Jack Sprat," who couldn't eat fat;
"Miss Muffet," who eats only curds and whey:
"Mr. Nobody," who eats everything we say

we never do. "Old Mother Hubbard"
living there in her shoe.
Although the child loves these verses,
she treasures most the quatrains of music singing

what she wants most to do: swing so high
she will never come back.
"How do you like to go up in a swing?
Up in the air so blue? Oh, I do think

it is the pleasantest thing
Ever a child can do."
The child knows that on her own swing
in her backyard she skims over the flat ground

and rises only slightly above an ordinary home.
The swing-set is rusty, imperfect, and
doesn't go "Up in the air and over the wall,
Till I can see so wide,

Rivers and trees and cattle and all,
Over the country side."
Why won't *her swing* let her take leave of
the world? Why does she go on playing as if
some swing might someday be the one she stroked
so much in her illustrated book?

II

When she's forty, for the first time she sees
England's hedgerows and garden-walls.
Are they the remains of her storybook pictures?
This May in an oceanside town she finds

an English manor house with its blooming May garden
high on a cliff looking out at the sea:
remnant of her childhood vision come true?
A long-roped, girl-laden, high-rising

out-over-the-ocean-and-not-coming-
back-again sublime perfection: *The Swing*.

III

In a hurried hovering above the place
she'd been that rainy Devon morning
the sea stretched out, beyond her, gray and so
impenetrable. The town, curled cat-like,

sat at sea's shore. Below, near her, the grass
from Sunday morning's rain . . . and her own son
sliding down slides he loves far more than swin
She says to herself those lines she once loved,

"Up in the air and down."

A WOMAN'S REPORT

I

Symmetric

Nightmares: my niece in pieces in a mud puddle.
Then I'm arrested for being "Unclean"
No member of my family is whole. All severed, irregular.

In a dream
he comes to me from all sides. Robed
in fire, filling my white-caladium
garden, he says, "You are Jacob.

You loathed Esau. I will make you
symmetric again." As I flee, he
pursues me, saying,

> "I am what
> I am.
> I am a rag man:
>
> the second coming,
> the dark self--renamed, returned."

II

Whole

Once in my dreams
He was a white-robed Galilean,
the millennium's double-crossed man.
He said He would restore.
Last night
I reached God again:
an old, bent East Indian--
hushed, gauze-clad, poor.

She said,

             "You're touching my altar.
             Turn."

RIVER TRAIL RIDE

It's a slow Sunday in Mississippi.
November. She sits on an old split fence.
Gold leaves are muted by a low, gray sky.
Fields are silent. It will be dark soon.

It seems a mere hour since she grew up here.
She can't recall orange hardwood like these
mingled with pine, sumac on all roadsides,
nor the "Bogue Chitto" River with live oaks

bending down to her with gray hair. Dry oak leaves.
Pine needles lie on the ground. She wants to say,
Nothing has fallen better than this.
She knows tomorrow the river will continue

cold, swift in its white sandy bend.
Now husband, two-year-old son in red flannel shirt,
green wool stretch-hat and blonde hair
trot toward her. Woods give them back

to begin again. Late mosquitos make her itch. Horseless,
in the old, Chevy truck at dark they drive on.

FOR MIRINDA

My six-year-old son once lay in cradles
by black babies, Indians, Indonesians.
His first trusted friend was dark as rich dirt.
His ebony-haired English nanny had fled Iran.

He would find it odd, my old friend Mirinda,
mother's maid's child, how we have to hide in the ▌
together--both fenced. At three we celebrate hues:
salmon clouds are as magic as skies or as skins.

At four we find nasturtiums taste yellow and orange.
Poppies smell red or pink. When five comes, I'm too
you too Negro for kindergarten.
We teach ourselves "Look and See":

your mother irons white sheets for my mother,
fifty cents for all day. Mama hand-washes them in th▌
Alchemists, you and I see sheets as tents,
wind-flapping on the line. We run in and out of star

treasure their stiffness as if it is gold.
In 1947, my baby sister has diapers to sudse
twice a week. Then it's '48;
I can't keep you. We turn six, go to school.

Lines to laundries. You grow up in Mississippi
just as I do.
Do you remember the *How and Why* book of stories
my mommy read both of us

while your mammy pressed, sipped ice water, waited,
drip-mopping her sweat?
My son has our pages,
now his, in Houston.

He knows nothing of history
or of how and why.
He's not seen that even people are prey.
He will grow toward knowledge, Mirinda: our inheritance.

Now his friends are Tursheeca, Sarah, Minasha, Albert--
sheet-like and inky children.
If I asked you what you've become
in forty-three years, lost sister,

if you sent me answers or echoes,
they'd mount into images like those in the album
mother has willed me.
No snapshots of us were ever clicked on black and white.

So I see you, Mirinda,
from my memory of you and me.

SITE OF A PISHKUN*

It isn't the red rocks hissing that
cause an Indian Pishkun to
scare me so.

It isn't the fact that no snakes crawl.
(Only space and vast absence eat
their own tails--

acrosss the cold, dry, frozen plateau.)
It isn't just that my vision
sees all waste

as one or that this has been holy
ground. It isn't that I look out at
nothingness

and am afraid.
                    It is that at last
I will not drive all wildness

like bison off cliffs. Now, since we turned
South from Highway 90, years ago,
just to see it

one snowless cold February,
piles of old buffalo bones lodge
still in the dust

beneath ancient cliffs. I go on plodding
down there with shovel and pick, digging
my blessed demons back.

*In the ancient pishkuns of the American Indians of the Great Plains, a shaman sat underneath a cliff performing incantations while men ran bison off the cliff to obtain meat and skins for the winter. Women attended to the dead bison, cutting the animals up and drying the meat and skins. There was a great waste in the ritual since more bison were killed than were needed each season. This poem is based on the remains of such a site outside Bozeman, Montana.

PEGASUS WINDING

Sixty-cent carnival tickets we buy
at a cellulite doll-lady's white shack.
She wolfs salami with mustard and bread.
Her helper sets us on plastic horses
whose tin music breaks. It's too cold for
lilac time. The entire carnival stinks.

We cross the banks of the falls into the
rain-soaked park. Listen to *this* carousel!
Here sinless gardens collect the simple
around them. The temple's light-dome is covered
in glass--a covenant ark saying,
"I will not leave you alone or forget

your passion for heavenly rides."
We follow the hand-carved, solid-wood horses,
prancing in air. Their backs boast jeweled saddles
Eyes glow and return our stares. On Pegasus,
not needing brass rings, we float
in Eden: round and round and round.

SEEING THE DESERT GREEN

The coarse, wooden forty-foot cross
has stood here on this hill since my childhood.
We cousins foot-raced up to it like crusaders,
called it "home."
Crucifixion haunted the invisible "snipes" we hunted here.
I reach it again, huffing.
Its rood still shadows the town just below.

There, in one wire-fenced yard,
Grandmother combed each inch of surface
for me to savor sweetness of sweetpeas,
the dry smell of geraniums in July
(so unlike wet aromas in gardens "back East"
where I lived in lushness all year).
Mother's mother migrated West,
raised flowers from prayer-rich dirt without top soil.

Few knew money here.
Out of last night, I heard a young woman
who lives with the rough-neck on the dust street cry
"Won't somebody save me?"
Neon signs just down the block
blinked the blue message my forebears clung to:
"Jesus Saves."

Not sleeping,
I climbed up the slopes to Taft's top,
asking why am I here,
hoping to see something new
on this same, old, black-pocked horizon.
Out there only wood oil-well pumps
stood hunched over, like witches brewing.
Now the San Joaquin Valley's

filled with those green patches.
But up here just before dawn,
the heat already smothers low Mohave hills.
Tumbleweeds flee like antelopes down banks.

Grandma gives her advice,
"Watch out for rattlesnakes."
She watched for miracles daily,
and every other year
Mama, Daddy, my sister and I were the miraculo
driving southwest 2,000 miles through barrenness.

At seven o'clock I'm back down
in Aunt Virginia's sparse, sprinkled trees
seeking an answer:
Have souls been saved by such drought and dust
I think of Christ in his forty-day desert trial.
Lonely, like Him, at noon I'll stop
at four parched graves in the plot--
grandmother, grandfather, uncle and aunt.

Seeing the desert green across the road,
I will wonder why I came back
and if irrigation pipes or Jesus nourishes
and saves the new scents of this forced farming:
alfalfa, Greek almonds, kiwis, apricots, citrus in s

South of here, behind "The Ridge,"
L.A. sprawls: "worldly sin,"
as Mamaw always said of San Francisco. . . .
But I've come here as a pilgrim,
crawling on bloody hands, knees.
St. Anthony, I am past forty.
Foolish like you, my desert fathers, mothers,
I wait in this dryness to drink.